Little Pink Plastic Babies

A book of poems

For permission request, contact Publisher at
hello@adaptivepressllc.com

Paperback ISBN: 978-1-965863-01-5
Ebook ISBN: 978-1-965863-00-8
Illustrated by P&G Management via Pexels, Pixabay, and Getty Images.
LCCN Number:2025933700

Adaptive Press LLC
12828 Willow Centre Drive Ste D
#92 Houston, TX 77066
www.adaptivepressllc.com

Little Pink Plastic Babies

A book of poems

David Romanda

Adaptive Press llc

To Atsuko

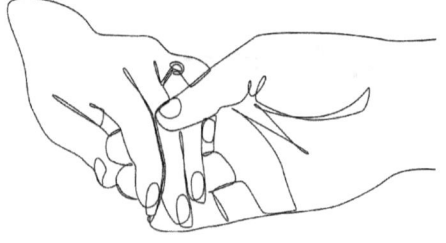

Content

Strange

And that was it.
He got up and grabbed
her tabby cat
and made for the door.
She grabbed a paring knife
and chased him
down the hallway
of her apartment building.
It was strange.
No one said anything.
It happened in near silence.
He ran with the cat. She chased him,
clutching a yellow-handled paring knife.

Truth

It won't ever come to it.
But if it does, you'd sell me out.
And I'd sell you out.
That's just how it is. No question.

David Romanda

Sunday Painter

Once he had adequate
time and adequate space,
he could no longer paint.
Not even on Sundays.

End

Trust is,
if you
think about it,
trust is a lot.
It's almost everything.
And I no longer trust you.

David Romanda

Smoke Break

"God, I'm horny," she whispered
into her cellphone. She was outside,
smoking, and I was going to get
a coffee. Reentering our building,
I heard her say into her phone,
"I love the way he cries and cries
when I tell him I can't live with him."

Note

You're never
out-of-your-skin-crazy-in-love
with the ones who can
love you back.

Abigail

I have my share
of troubles
like we all do.
But tonight, darling,
I remember you.
It was the way
you wrinkled your nose
when I asked you to dance
there beside that
loud-flowing river
on that beautiful early-autumn day.
We were children, but I think I loved you.
"Dance?" you said.
And the river carried our laughter away.

Finding Trouble

She follows the handsome
man in the pinstriped suit.
She's fifteen, twenty years
younger than him. But she can't resist.
He seems so familiar. Handsome.
From another time handsome.
She wants to know where he lives.
She wants to know what she can know
without making contact. He stops,
looks back over his shoulder.
"You don't want to do this," he says. "I'm a mistake."
Then, our heroine turns, and runs away.

Roses are Red

He had a series
of unsatisfactory
love affairs with
bored housewives

they gave him gifts
baked stuff
knitted things
one wrote him a poem

Roses are red
violets are blue
my husband's a creep
don't become one too

This Will Show Them

So angry
the little monkey
holds her breath
until she turns blue
they don't care if you end yourself
silly monkey
they don't care about you

Mad

She's holding
his hand
and suddenly
she stops
holding his hand

she forgot that she was mad

Scars

My new buddy invited me out
to dinner with his new wife.
We went to a Thai place and got
happy on Thai beer. My new
buddy's new wife started talking.
She said she used to cut herself.
"Sometimes, at night, I just
needed to see blood," she said.
Then she said, "Look at my wrists."
She held them up to show me.
They were scarred up pretty bad.
"Is it OK to touch?" I said.
She nodded, and I ran my fingertips
over the patchwork of scars
on her right wrist. My buddy never
invited me out with him and his wife again.

The Human Condition

Some people
like feeling trapped,
he says. Then,
Look, that was a joke.
Come on, I feel just
as stuck in my life
as you do in yours.
That's the Human Condition.
Can't you see that?
Can't you just be happy being human?

Life Is Boring

She tells me
she's writing a book
exploring boredom.
She's strangely passionate
about the topic. She's all
worked up. And then
I smell the whiskey on her breath.

David Romanda

Equality Equals Freedom

Slaughterbots need love too.
Don't laugh.
Don't you dare.
Love is love—and your need
is no greater than the Slaughterbot's.

She's Learned Her Lesson

While the hostess is seating them
in the fancy fusion restaurant,
she tells herself again and again,
mantra-like: remember the lies you tell,
remember the lies you tell, remember the lies you tell.

David Romanda

The Laundromat

I walked into the brightly lit laundromat
and found an older lady crying—her face puffy,
her nose running. "I'm sorry," I said, and turned to go.
"No, don't go," she said, "I'll tell you everything."

At the Jeweler's

This is the one,
she says. This ring,
she says. It can't be
any other. I was
born to wear this ring
on my finger.
You were born to buy
it for me. The man
asks the jeweler, skeptically,
How much?

David Romanda

Forget

She wants to forget
her husband,
she says.
She wants to forget
all the bad and
all the good.
I want to forget and
forget and
forget, she says,
with her mouth on my body.

Better Late Than Never

After twenty and a half years,
they're sure that they're not
sure they belong together.

David Romanda

Mirrors

She had this phase. She wouldn't look
in mirrors. Didn't want them around.
It was something superstitious,
something she'd thought up,
and believed in, but wouldn't explain.
This went on for six, maybe seven weeks.
And then she was fine with mirrors again.

Dear Laura

It's been such a long time.
Honestly, I don't know where to begin.
So, I won't begin.
Please stop calling my mother.

David Romanda

Now She Takes Pictures of Her Feet

One sunny day
she was
suddenly
empty of poetry

The Broken Bird Feeder

She wants it
and for that reason
I want it

David Romanda

Condoms Break

Cindy wanted
to call her baby girl
the Condom that Broke.
In the end, she named
the baby Courtney.

You Looked Good in Your Tight Sweater

When you hinted at marriage,
I took your hand and gently kissed

your ring finger. I shouldn't have
done that. And I apologize.

I was drunk and you looked good
in your tight sweater. And I was pissed off

at my girlfriend. Look, what I mean
to say is this—I'd like you to stop contacting me.

David Romanda

The Problem Is This

I can't find anything
I dislike about you.

And, to be brutally honest,
that scares me.

Missing

She has
a husband,
a kid,
a house,
and a car.
She works part time
at a non-profit,
a job she enjoys.
She likes her life,
but feels something
is missing.
She has no clue
what that something
might be.
But something
is missing.
Something is missing.

David Romanda

Can I Tell You Something?

I still think about you.
Mostly I'm hoping
you're unhappy.
Not sick or anything.
Just unhappy.
Let down by life.
Bored.
And yes, I'd take you back
in a second if you wanted me.

Over the Phone

You have nothing to say? she said.
(Silence.)
Do you still want me? she said.
I said, I thought I did, but now I'm really not sure.

David Romanda

The Ghostwriter

What she really
wants to write
are off-kilter haiku
about fake smiles
and bad breath
and yeast infections.

After

After she won
the prize, she was
stuck. "Now what?"

David Romanda

Waiting

He notices a woman
in torn up jeans
standing at the payphone
in the train station.
He sees her there morning
after morning after morning
in those torn up jeans.
Just standing there waiting.
And then one morning she's not there.

A House in the Mountains

Despite what others predicted,
their marriage lasted. They saved up
through the years and bought
a house in the mountains with a view
and half an acre of land. There's a pond
in back with a rowboat
and a little island with a one-room shack.
All of it is beautiful. Beyond beautiful.
But she keeps having these dreams.
She sees herself from above,
her body floating face-down at the pond's edge.

David Romanda

Victoria's Pig Died

From midnight to 4:00 a.m.,
Victoria cradled Snuffles in her arms,
"carrying him through the Shadow Realm
into the Light."

Now she wants a cat.

Duran Duran

We were sixteen,
maybe seventeen,
walking by the river,
and Heather said,
My best friend
killed himself
over there. She gestured
to a graveled parking area.
He came in the night, she said,
plugged up the muffler
with a bunch of socks,
rolled up the windows
and kept the car running.
The police found a Duran Duran
tape in the tape deck. And I was jealous of Heather.
Her life seemed so much larger than mine.
And it was.

David Romanda

Again

It's about waiting day in
and night out. It's waiting yawning
then waiting breathless. It's the waiting
for it to come again and knowing
it will not come again.

Warning

I always get a warning before
a seizure hits. Sometimes I hear a voice
or fucked up sounds in my head
(I heard angry-electric whispery orcs once).
Other times, I feel, for no reason,
like I'm going to puke.
I've gotten to the point where, if I feel strange,
I get down and lay flat on the ground.
I've done this on a crowded train,
at a shoe store,
at the supermarket.
I figure, "You're gonna end up on the ground anyway."

Punished

For the longest time,
Emma believed that God
would punish bad people,
but then she realized
that everyone gets punished,
one way or the other,
good or bad.

Dreaming Big

I remember
dreaming big
back before
our lives began.
Now I just
want to be alone
with my hand.

Routine

He was used to masturbating three times a day.
But now he's older and doesn't need to masturbate that often.
He continues doing it three times a day.

Can't Make It

I've got
plans
to stay home
and chase my tail.

David Romanda

Woman in a Yellow Dress Crying in the Condiments Aisle

Can I help? I asked.

She said, Yes.
But she pushed her cart slowly away.

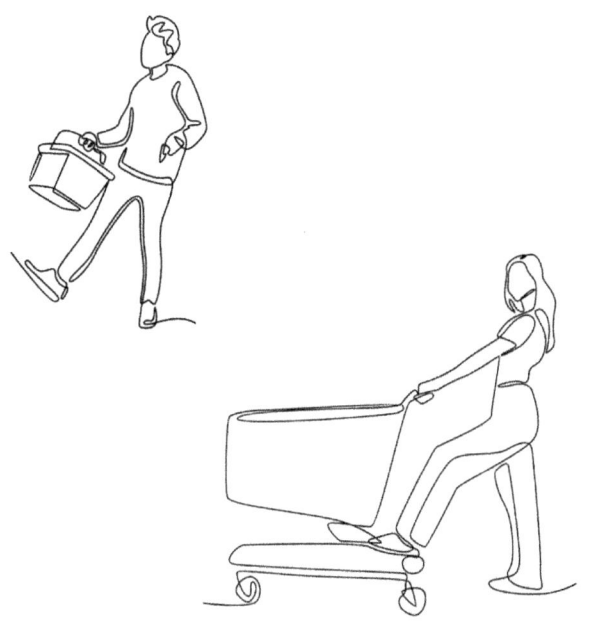

Stop

He picked up the phone
and thought it was his
dead mother. He felt her
presence, but it was
that prank caller again.
The one that says nothing,
with a dead mother's presence.
Mother, he writes in his
last letter to her, I want
you to stop calling. You're
gone. And I want to
stop writing you letters.
You're gone. I need to stop holding on.

Goodbye, Jane

I was in bad shape.
Drunk on champagne,
crying. I couldn't make
eye contact with Jane.
I suggested we both
kill ourselves so we
could be happy. The next
morning, on the train,
returning to my wife,
I wondered what I was like
in the middle of that madness.

David Romanda

Bad Day

Is it just a bad day
or week
or month
or year?
Or is it, maybe, a bad life?

Money

We were in grade six, Ryan and me. We'd go around
the neighborhood with a bucket and two sponges and some
dish soap and try to wash cars. We charged ten bucks a pop
if people asked, but we preferred to let people pay what they
wanted (some people would pay fifteen or twenty bucks, but
most paid four or five). One afternoon we were hanging out
at Ryan's place, drinking Coke, and Ryan's mom asked me
if I wanted to wash her car. I said, Sure. I washed the car.
Ryan stayed inside. Ryan's mom came out and carefully
inspected the work I'd done. She was satisfied, paid me
twelve bucks. I felt weird about the situation. I was happy
to have the cash, but I felt weird. My friendship with Ryan
shifted after that. We were never as close. Sure, we still
washed cars and made money together. But something
changed.

Little Pink Plastic Babies

It was confusing. Dad woke us up before the sun was in the sky. This never happened. Dad never woke us up and we never got up before it was light out. But my sister and I were in elementary school and we didn't really ask questions. We had cereal and apple juice and packed our knapsacks for school, but we didn't go to school that morning. We drove over the bridge and into the city. We parked and walked to some sort of hospital. It was starting to get light out. People were standing outside the hospital with signs. They were singing. They held chains with little pink plastic babies dangling rom them. Inside, mom and dad and my sister and me sat and waited. Then mom was called in. Dad took us downstairs into a cafeteria. Dad got coffee, but he didn't drink any of it. My sister and I had grape juice. Dad seemed tired When I asked him what was going on, he said, "Everything's going to be fine." Mom came down into the cafeteria after a long while. She didn't look at my sister or me. She took dad's hand and we all got up. Dad drove us to a Greyhound bus station. Mom and dad got out of the car. Dad opened the trunk and got out mom's suitcase. My sister and I just waited in the car. We could tell it wasn't time for us to move.

Then mom and dad came back to the car after a while. Dad put mom's suitcase back in the trunk. "You're both going to school now," Dad said. It sounded as if his voice was somehow broken. I knew it wasn't time to ask questions. We were dropped off at school. And that was that.

David Romanda

Divorce

The words
didn't sound right
coming out
of my mouth
but I was past
the point
of no return

Chess

When I started to win
dad no longer
wanted
to play with me

David Romanda

Dreams

When we knew grandpa was dying
(dying for sure), I felt guilty talking
about the future. He had travelled
the world, and throughout my life
we talked about the places I wanted
to see, the places he had seen, and those
he would have seen. We talked about
our dreams (though we never called them
dreams). I could no longer tell grandpa
my goals. I felt so guilty. And, of course,
I couldn't ask about his. What dreams
do the dying have other than getting well?

Sometimes I Can't Sleep

On those nights, I think of my dad.
I remember attempting to sneak out
to meet a girlfriend in the middle
of the night and getting caught.
Dad was sitting on his recliner
in his bathrobe. Just sitting there
in the darkness. What was going on
in his head? What are you doing? he said.
I'm going to meet my girlfriend
from school, I said. Then I asked,
What are you doing? Don't wake up
your mother when you come home, he said.

David Romanda

Once

In a dream,
my dead grandma
handed me a key.

"It will open
any lock," she said.
"But you can only use it once."

Blue Guitar

On her deathbed,
my grandmother's
last words to me were,
"Don't give up the guitar."
I stopped playing
not long after her death,
and haven't struck a chord
in twenty years.

David Romanda

Fertility Clinic

Me
and my wife
drinking
water
out of paper cups

David Romanda

Bad News

When my father
gave me the bad news
all I could say was
"I love you." I was just a kid,
but I knew love was the best thing
I had to offer when confronted with disaster.

Happy Belated Birthday

Now that you've fully and properly
apologized (thanks!), I thought it might
be appropriate to wish you a very
Happy Belated Birthday!

David Romanda

An Afternoon Walk

The shouting lunatic
catches my eye,

or did I catch hers?
She stops shouting,

her face softens.
She smiles, a gold tooth

gleaming. The world
is ending, she says.

Yes, I say.
And I continue on my way.

Change My Life

Woke up this morning
with the notion
that I was going
to change my life.
Got dressed
and went out for a run.
Got back home a mess.
My knee and back killing me.

David Romanda

Running Out of Material

The young poet is
running out of material.
"I'm not even forty, and I feel spent.
I'm done, a goner." Then, "Thank Heavens."
He gets cancer.

Make Me Healthy Again

They poison me
via slow drip I.V.
then they blast me
with radiation
to kill the growth
in my brain
to make me healthy again

David Romanda

Secrets

I'd heard
somewhere
that secrets
keep us young.
One way
or another
I've woven all
of my secrets
into poems.
And I'm not
aging gracefully.

Ethics

Do you or do you not
inform your fellow man
that he's having an unruly
nose hair crisis?

David Romanda

Satisfied

She wasn't
satisfied with
the way
her novel
turned out,
but then
she realized
she wasn't
satisfied with
anything in
her life.
"You know what?
The novel's done,"
she said
to herself.
And she felt good.

Made in His Image

Why don't
we imagine
a hunchbacked God?

David Romanda

His Name Was Magawa

This rat that sniffed out landmines was awarded a prize
for heroism. He very recently died of old age. I was
thinking it would be fitting for him to go out in a landmine
blast or something. But no. Thank you for your service, hero
rat.

Under Her Breath

I asked for extra napkins.
The girl looked at me,
rolled her eyes and grabbed
a bunch of extra napkins
(maybe twenty or thirty),
and held them up in the air.
Then she pushed them into the bag,
held the bag up in the air,
and then passed it over
the counter to me. I took the bag,
said "Thanks," and turned to leave.
I could swear she muttered,
"I want to piss on your grave."
I turned around.
"Have a good day, sir," she said,
in a cheery voice, without smiling.

David Romanda

This Is Our Last Letter to You

It is unfortunate
that you didn't find
our assistant manager's
smile sufficiently "warm."
He is only human,
like you, and perhaps
his wife busted his chops
the night before, and he just
couldn't put that extra
oomph into his smile.
We consider this matter closed.
Please don't write again, as we will not reply.

Help

He's seventeen. He goes to the family doctor
and tells her he's not happy. She gives him
a multiple-choice questionnaire to fill out.
He fills it out, then she checks it, and says,
You're moderately depressed. The doctor wants
to check his thyroid. There's no issue with his thyroid.
Then she asks if he wants to maybe talk with
a counsellor. He says no. Then she prescribes pills.
The pills make our hero sluggish and emotionally blunted.
He stops taking the pills and doesn't return to the doctor.

David Romanda

Houseplants

I wonder
what the
houseplants
think of me
and my wife.
Do they
like us?
Or are they
silently
awaiting
their chance
to smother us
in our sleep?

The Poem Writes Itself

When the poem writes itself
you're either writing shit
or bordering on genius

David Romanda

Maybe I Shouldn't Do That

Sometimes
I wave goodbye
to myself
in the mirror

In the Past

I basically
drank to forget

now that I stopped drinking
all I do is remember

David Romanda

Forgiveness

It's like making
a cup of tea for an old friend

you do it
without being asked

Chance of a Lifetime

He cold calls her,
opening with this line:
"Listen, you have
to believe me, this is
one-hundred percent
not a scam." She listens
politely for about thirty
seconds and says she doesn't
have money to invest.
He stops. Waits.
And then he says, "Um,
could I maybe take you out
for a coffee or something?"

David Romanda

The Latest Book

Are these poems good
because the poet is famous,
or is the poet famous
because these poems are good?

P.S.

When you die,
your cats will eat you.

David Romanda

Acknowledgements

Adelaide Literary Magazine: "Equality Equals Freedom," "Truth"

Alba: "Mirrors"

Duck Head Journal: "An Afternoon Walk," "Change my Life," "Money"

Great Ape: "Ethics"

The Moth: "His Name Was Magawa," "Victoria's Pig Died"

Nebo: "This Will Show Them"

Noon: "Secrets"

North Dakota Quarterly: "Dreams," "Warning"

Perceptions Magazine: "She's Learned Her Lesson," "Sometimes I Can't Sleep"

Popshot Quarterly: "Duran Duran"

Postscript Magazine: "Strange"

Riddle Fence: "Little Pink Plastic Babies"

Rio Grande Review: "Houseplants," "Scars"

Route 7 Review: "Abigail"

Yolk: "Smoke Break"

Index

David Romanda

About the author
David Romanda was born in Kelowna, British Columbia.

He studied literature and psychology at the University of the Fraser Valley, where he wrote poems and articles for the university newspaper, The Cascade. Romanda graduated from university in 2006 and left Canada to teach English in Japan. Today, he calls Kawasaki City home. He is married to biologist Atsuko Tanimura. Romanda's work has appeared in publications around the globe such as Columbia Review, Cordite Poetry Review, Poetry Ireland Review, Poetry Salzburg Review, and PRISM international.

Romanda's poem "We Really Like Your Writing" was included in Best Canadian Poetry 2021.

Romanda is the author of one limited-edition chapbook, I'm Sick of Pale Blue Skies and one poetry collection, Why Does She Always Talk About Her Husband?

Romanda has been interviewed by PANK and Prolific Pulse.

Check Romanda out online: www.romandapoetry.com